GOOD ACTORS

GOOD ACTORS
sommer browning

birds, llc
minneapolis, new york, raleigh, washington d.c.

birdsllc.com

Copyright © 2021 Sommer Browning

Cover art "Man Drawing" by Liliana Porter
Cover design by Hollis Duncan

First edition, 2021

Library of Congress Control Number: 2021935511

ISBN: 978–1–7346321–0–1

Printed in the United States of America

CONTENTS

... it's only in the movies that it's easy.
John Cassavetes

It's just language.
Jeanne Liotta

Curtain opens to reveal a ~~theater~~ meadow.

Good Actors

I want to make a movie before I turn 45

About two characters exchanging money.

I give them directions. I say to them, *Earnestly.*

As if holding grilled cheeses,

They push the money into each other's hands.

I call out, *Reluctantly.* They look down

And say, *Goddamnit, this is the last time, Ray.*

And weave it between their fingers.

They are good actors. So I say,

Hopefully. They blink and gaze into their hands

Like into a new baby. *Angrily,* I say. They gnaw

The money to confetti. I tell them,

As if in mourning. And the money fevers

Down their wrists. And now, *Like a bank.*

They fist and throw it like garbage.

And a forest? Now a forest? Like seed

They sow it. *You're doing very well,* I say.

They drop it at my feet.

Exuberantly, I say. They remove their clothing.

Lovingly, I say. They move toward me.

They are such good actors.

They turn off the camera.

If you tell me which *Twilight Zone* episode you remember best, I can tell you what your problem is.

Little People. Astronaut on foreign planet finds colony of tiny people. Treated like a god. Goes maniacal. Stomps on LP. Giant astros arrive and stomp on him.

Your problem is: You cannot reconcile your desire to believe in something greater than yourself with your doubt that something greater than you exists.

Thank You

Thank you, Moms Mabley.

Thank you, Moms Mabley and Phyllis Diller.

Thank you, Moms Mabley, who ran away at 14 to join a vaudeville troupe, and Phyllis Diller and Joan Rivers.

Thank you, Moms Mabley and Phyllis Diller, who started doing stand-up at 37, and Joan Rivers and Carol Burnett.

Thank you, Moms Mabley, who came out at 27 in 1921, and Phyllis Diller and Joan Rivers, who kept a note from Lenny Bruce that said, *They're wrong, you're right,* in her bra for years, and Carol Burnett.

Thank you, Moms Mabley, who came out at 27 in 1921, and Phyllis Diller and Joan Rivers, who bombed every night for two years, and Carol Burnett, who said, *There's laughter in everything.*

Thank you, Moms Mabley and Phyllis Diller, who started doing stand-up at 37, and Joan Rivers and Carol Burnett, who said, *There's laughter in everything,* and Bea Arthur.

Thank you, Moms Mabley and Phyllis Diller, who started doing stand-up at 37, and Joan Rivers, who claims she was the first female host of the *Tonight Show,* but so does Florence Henderson, Phyllis Newman, and Della Reese, and who really cares anyway, and Carol Burnett and Bea Arthur, whose TV character, Maude, chose to get an abortion at age 47 in 1972.

Thank you, Moms Mabley, who gave birth to six people, and Phyllis Diller, who gave birth to five people, and Joan Rivers, who gave birth to one person, and Carol Burnett, who gave birth to three people, and Bea Arthur, who mothered two people.

Thank you.

If you tell me which *Twilight Zone* episode you remember best, I can tell you what your problem is.

"Eye of the Beholder" (I already believe my problem is with conformity).

Your problem is: You doubt your knowledge.

Denver is Home to the World's First Quiznos

In Alice Notley's *Waltzing Matilda* the narrator reads a friend's poems, contends with the ambivalences of marriage, tends to sick children, gets hammered, makes an ass of herself, worries about making an ass of herself, reads the news, frets about money. Good god, am I describing my life or a book of poems? This book was published in 1981. I was published in 1976.

Lately when I sit down to write it's a firework. (This essay will be an admirable example! Also, I do not write of Quiznos in it.) A thousand threads spiraling out of a teeny, tiny, imperceptible, barely pulsing center a.k.a. my brain. I don't know if the diversity of these threads makes sense, sense is likely too haughty of a goal anyway. But they seem to affect each other. Take the way I recently injected Fred Sandback into a fantasy [us making love next to *Untitled. 1967.]* with my new lover. Or the way accidentally no-showing my therapist on Monday is directly connected to my inability to get my daughter's and my new telescope aligned. So far, we have seen the impenetrable fabric of night, really up close, and a neighbor's garage, really up close.

A few days ago, on a November day, Alice Notley tweeted [yes for real] that she is having a birthday. Today, on this November day, I randomly opened *Grave of Light: New and Selected Poems, 1970–2005* and read the poem, "The Trouble With You Girls." It begins:

> In the chair covered with shawls
> I'm wearing my favorite red shirt
> Maybe it's November near my birthday, sun
> On my shoulder and coffee too in what cup chipped;

"...coffee too in what cup chipped." Just damn. This phrase is a song. Later:

> Day's lovely before I'm
> Too many thoughts, I've become content this year;

Content? Or content? How wonderful to be both.

And running in the background of her thoughts, Ted is talking at or to her. She admits she isn't listening. She answers the question, what's a person for?

I think it's
Partly to be with a plant.

Two nights ago, I watched *3 Faces* by Jafar Panahi at the Denver Film Festival. It was very good. My friend Andrew told me Panahi once had to sneak a film out of Iran in a birthday cake because the government banned him from making films, but he made one anyway. *3 Faces* is about a dozen things. One of those things seems to be the human need to create despite horrible consequences, or, if I were a film critic, "the enduring power of self-expression."

Notley writes in her poem: *I don't know what I'm for.*

Ted, in her poem, talks so much about objects. He mentions chairs and things to drink and sunshine and coffee and money and asses and cigarettes and Pepsi and the newspaper and doughnuts and ... philosophy. It is funny to place philosophy into his litany of things, but it becomes an object. He says in the poem "You have no philosophy" which sounds to me like half, *Dude, you're out of toilet paper,* and half, *Yakkity yakkity yak.*

In an exquisite example of bibliomancy (bibliomancy is always exquisite, maybe?), "The Trouble With You Girls" is also about "the enduring power of self-expression." Go figure. Ted's standing in for what the power must endure; in this poem it is money, patriarchy, lofty ideals about the artist, the outside world of news and current events, the body's needs.

A couple of weeks ago, my friend Julia asked me to speak to her students about a few poems I wrote. Sometimes I don't know who I am until I say it out loud. This time, a student asked me if I believe in the angels and muses that some poets and artists say speak through them. I told them I have never had such an angel, but I believe in other people's angels. I also said, almost as if in warning, that the existence of these angels doesn't let us off the hook. That there is a lot of work we must do to prepare ourselves for the arrival of angels. Gotta fill yourself up with stuff angels like.

Then I said, and this scared the hell out of me: *I've been preparing for these angels my whole life.*

If this is true, then getting a DUI a million years ago and breaking my sister's horse cookie out of jealousy another million years ago and crying in front of my boss last month and divorcing and mooning the Grand Canyon and staying on the phone for hours with a sick friend and cleaning my mother's house on my hands and knees and sneaking into *Lethal Weapon II* and watching my child do the Floss and being a librarian and forgetting to buy deodorant last night was all in preparation for the arrival of angels. It seems impossible but, it was, it is. It's a terrifying relief, frankly. I don't have to write "prepare for angels" on my to-do list. In fact! (And this is wonderful!) I'll rename my to do list: Prep for Angels.

Sometimes, I'm a lot more Ted than I think.

If you tell me which *Twilight Zone* episode you remember best, I can tell you what your problem is.

The old lady is tormented by US Astronauts (sorry, spoilers).

Your problem is: The impossibility of aligning one's morals with one's needs and desires causes you suffering.

Great Things from the Department of Transportation

My mother desires to track my location on her phone.

My mother announces that she's "latex intolerant."

My mother is horrified that the children's cartoon character Caillou is bald.

My mother to the server at a terrible restaurant: *I don't want a box—I want a flamethrower.*

One's mother might be the most famous person one knows.

My mother says, *There is no Denny's, only Zuul.*

My mother on penises and traffic cones: *On occasion they're both orange, aren't they?*

The young lungs of my mother fill with fine particulate matter on the streets of Clairton, PA.

My mother on the X-rated hypnotist: *He was only concerned with having the hypnotized persons act sexually stupid.*

One night in the 1970s, in the Mojave Desert, my mother ceases to feel apart from the world.

My mother pays my sister and me $40 each to not have birthday parties.

My mother's soulmate is not my father but her dog, Six.

The only thing I don't like about John Wick is that he never washes his hair.

My mother's father, a bipolar beer distributor, laughs at least once that I know of because it echoes through me for 40 years.

On the whole my mother likes Miranda July's novel, *The First Bad Man,* but could have done without the sex parts.

I listen to my mother tell my child a story as if I were my own daughter.

My mother tells me there were some skanks on *America's Next Top Model.*

My mother asks, *Didn't someone famous say, "What doesn't kill you makes you stronger?"*

My mother prays for her children every night.

My mother prays for children every night.

I bet you never thought you'd marry, have a baby, and get divorced before you're 40, she tells me.

My mother expects great things from the Department of Transportation.

If you tell me which *Twilight Zone* episode you remember best, I can tell you what your problem is.

"The Monsters are Due on Maple Street."

Your problem is: Reconciling the feeling of unfreedom that routine possesses with your need for order.

Historicity

Best ending to this story, Ben, is for me to finish the movie.

Best ending to this story, Ben, is the thud of the script hitting your front
porch when I deliver it to you.

The drama of that thud like the tomb closing, Ben, on Jesus, Ben,
Jesus Christ, Ben, a few days before he comes back, Ben,

How Jesus came crawling back, Ben,
Asking his apostles for forgiveness, Ben, for calling them addicts, Ben,
For telling them how great they were, what good mothers
They were, Ben, how their careers were really gaining

Momentum, Ben, for telling them they were his forever
People, Ben, then calling them sociopaths, Ben.

Forgiveness for that.

Best ending to this story, Ben, is our movie winning that prize, Ben,
And me telling you and you having to say, *Thanks. Thanks for supplying
the perfect ending to our story,*

Sommer,
Ben,

That's the best way to end this story & make the stars cum all over the
galaxy, Ben,

All over every planet, Ben, watch cum streak through the atmosphere of
some dead planet, Ben,

Watch it burn off in blurs, Ben, watch one seed escape and
Land on that dry, rocky landscape, maybe Mars, Ben, maybe it melts,
maybe it bursts, Ben.

Carbon,
Ben.

Making stains all over the face of that planet, Ben, a seed, Ben, breaks
Open and releases a blueprint, Ben, that cute
Little tail sperm have, Ben, that potential energy, the stupid
Spark of which the planet's lone molecule of Mars-water has been
dreaming, Ben, that molecule looking up from its parched porch into the
forever black at the blue, so blue, Blue Earth spinning and needy.

Ben.
Listen.

The water and the sperm fall in love and, Ben,
That's how babies are made.
The baby roots, two into one, Ben,
It clutches the desiccated earth (but Mars), Ben, and wheezes itself
upright into a cacophonous, impossible storm of scabs,
It wheezes *Life,*
It says, *Life,* Ben,
Ben, it murmurs *Mercy,*
It says, *Mercy,* Ben,
Ben, it says, *We,* Ben,
Ben, it screams *We.*

If you tell me which *Twilight Zone* episode you remember best, I can tell you what your problem is.

The one where the dude keeps feeding the fortune telling machine.

Your problem is: You vacillate between embodying two distinct ideals of yourself.

Sex

PERSON 1

Yes?

PERSON 2

Yes.

If you tell me which *Twilight Zone* episode you remember best, I can tell you what your problem is.

The one in the diner with people stranded and turning on one another. The waiter has three eyes.

Your problem is: You believe in the validity of multiple perspectives—even oppositional ones—in others, but you do not allow this generosity for yourself.

To Drunk To Fuck

And now what do I do =?=
Too drunk to write'

Too drunk to type
Do I try to din a eer===pserosbn>'

I am only drunk enogh to type
No one to ruck'

Bukowsku

Aare you an asnswer?'

No youalways seemed srukned wnought
To fuck
But I am not
I am too crunk t oevven fuck

I will take off m y dresss
And then will I ven want to typeanymore

Provalbly not
Too tired'

There is no man here
There is cothing in the washing machine

I don't hav e energy to '
Put it in in the dryer

But you bukowski
The lust'

But you rimabaud'
The bukowski'

I play naiu=ma
Coltrane

I am alone
I wanted ot love a oet

Wanted to love a poet
Wanted to laove a oemt

This seems true
I will watcha wmovie and
T will make me m elss lovely
Maube an Altman

If you tell me which *Twilight Zone* episode you remember best, I can tell you what your problem is.

The one with the dolls/people in the garbage can.

Your problem is: Resolving what is possible with what is probable causes you to suffer.

Super Bowl

I knew today would be special,
but not eating-wings-alone-in-an-Asian-fusion-restaurant special.

If you tell me which *Twilight Zone* episode you remember best, I can tell you what your problem is.

The couple finds themselves in a realistic but fake town and gradually discovers they are the pets of a giant alien child. Esp. when she touches the squirrel.

Your problem is: What others want for you masquerades as your own desire.

All I Have to Do is Act Naturally

Me: Hi.

The Void:

Me: Hi.

The Void:

Me: Hi.

The Void:

Me: Hi.

The Void:

Me: Hi.

The Void:

Me: Hi.

The Void:

Me: Hi.

The Void:

Me: Hi.

If you tell me which *Twilight Zone* episode you remember best, I can tell you what your problem is.

The one where the guy thinks he is in heaven but is in hell.

Your problem is: You believe there is a difference between what makes you happy and what you pursue, and this causes misery.

Do You Have an Extra Cigarette?

Have you ever heard Aram Saroyan read his poem "Biography"?[1] It is a poem in which he recites every year from his birth to the current year in his usual steady, calm cadence. I'm a bit fascinated with this poem; I seem to bring it up often. It really can't be beat. It's a pure poem. I heard him read it in 2007 (I think) at Poet's House in New York. There are a hundred things to say about the poem, how the simplicity of it belies the fact that it describes something huge (i.e., a human life), how it disrupts the idea of a poem—a list poem in particular, how cheeky it is, how the poem must change every year and so, in a way, it is unpublishable (if we think of publication as an unfuckwithable record, certainly Lyn Hejinian doesn't [see her various updates of *My Life*]).

Anyway, when I listened to this poem I felt many things. I had an initial laugh near the beginning after hearing five or six chronological numbers and realizing he must be reciting the years from his birth year and how clever that is since the poem is called, simply "Autobiography!"[2] And then I felt a knowing, in-on-the-joke feeling, as he continued to recite the years. And as it continued (I'm not making an age joke here), I settled into two feelings between which I vacillated. The first was *Okay, I get it, Aram*—not boredom but surety, like how it might feel to know the future. The second was a kind of joy, an oh-hell-he's-really-going-to-go-through-with-it feeling. The combination of these feelings made me laugh out loud a time or two, smile quietly, and fidget. These feelings are what happens when I confront excess, repetitive excess, in art. It's a particular kind of humorous feeling.

It might be unfair to choose Saroyan since he is a master of this repetitive excess, consider his poem "Crickets." But there are many poets who do this, and many artists, and, of course, your Uncle Terry who repeats his jokes until they are busted up shards at your feet. In this way, Uncle Terry is an artist.

---

[1] Have I? I have never been certain of its title.
[2] Between footnotes I emailed Aram Saroyan and the poem is actually titled: "Autobiography."

(In a 2007 *Armenian Reporter* interview, Saroyan clarifies that it was Robert Duncan, not George Plimpton, who chose Saroyan's "lighght" for the NEA award.[3] And an ANGEL conveyed this choice to Duncan, an angel! It is pure joy to know this. Plus, how amazingly excessive is lighght, righght?)

What is the relationship between humor and excess? (Choose the best subtitle.)

> · A thirty-part opinion series Sommer will tackle in five-hundred words.
> · A nine times failed AWP panel proposal.
> · Tonight at 11.

I don't know. Frankly, I hate opinions; opinions cause a lot of pain. I also hate when someone asks you, *Do you have an extra cigarette?* Because cigarettes are things that can never be extra.

Maybe try to define excess? Like in a sentence?

Life is merely an excess of life, a pessimist might say. While death is an excess of death, his unbearable brother might add. It is very hard to please a pessimist, let alone two.

Addiction is excess depending on which side of it you're on.

Power is always in a state of excess while there is nothing excessive about love.

3 Lola Koundakjian, "Questions to Aram Saroyan," *Armenian Reporter,* December 8, 2007, C17–C19.

If you tell me which *Twilight Zone* episode you remember best, I can tell you what your problem is.

Number 12 looks just like you. I remember talking about this show with you, not that episode, but the show in general.

Your problem is: The gulf you perceive between beauty and truth causes you pain.

Yes

for men

Sure.
Yeah.
Totally.
No problem.
Anything you want.
Of course.
Surely.
Certainly.
Uh huh.
You got it.
You're on.
Right-O.
Okay.
Affirmative.
Positively.
Absolutely.
Gladly.
Forsooth.
I'll do it.
Fine.

Agreed.
Approved.
Is the Pope Catholic?
Let's do it.
With pleasure.
You bet.
Yah.
By all means.
Leave it to me.
Okie dokie.
Alright.
Yup.
For sure.
Hell, yes.
Verily.
Aye.
Roger.
Very well.
Indeed.
Count me in.

If you tell me which *Twilight Zone* episode you remember best, I can tell you what your problem is.

The one with the thing on the wing of the plane.

The airplane wing one.

I choose the one with gremlins on the airplane.

The one with the monster on the plane. "Monster at 20,000 Feet." I flew a lot as a child, and that one really freaked me out.

That one with the guy on the plane that sees hallucinations on the wing!!

"Nightmare at 20,000 Feet:" the one with the monster on the wing of the plane.

The one where the guy sees a monster on the plane wing, and no one believes him.

Your problem is: You are in conflict, because you believe in justice but also think the world is meaningless.

The Deer

The deer—

    whose homeschooled deerlings call the dead telephone poles
    who bully the fences decategorizing the high desert
    who swallow the hysterical to become sluts
    who spit to don flickering halos
        the glint of which pry out hunters' retinas, thin cloud of wet
        microscopes

The deer somehow—

        not for lack but of trying to lack
        too near us, and so frequently
        are given rooms
        branded gentility
        but how we've won is when the deer absent themselves
        and leak privately

        —know I am a mother.

If you tell me which *Twilight Zone* episode you remember best, I can tell you what your problem is.

Man loves to read, wishes he could be alone to do so, immediately breaks eyeglasses.

The one where the man wanted to be alone to read and then was and broke his glasses!

"Time Enough at Last."

Burgess Meredith is a post-apocalyptic survivor, and his glasses break at the end.

Omg yes. The library one! Where he breaks his glasses!

That's easy. It's the one where the guy who loves to read gets locked in the bank vault, when the rest of the world is wiped out. He can finally read anything he wants any time he wants. But then he trips and shatters his glasses.

"Time Enough At Last."

The one where the guy just wants to read all the books but is always distracted by outside sources, then survives a nuclear bomb and has the time to read, but breaks his glasses and he can't see a thing.

Burgess Meridith stepping on his glasses. "All the time in the world..."

The library fellow who only wants to read, facing apocalypse with his reading glasses shattered.

Bad Sex

I tried to pee on a man once. We thoroughly discussed it—both what it might feel like to pee on someone and to be peed upon. We systematically took off our clothes; we probably even folded them. We positioned ourselves in the bathtub exactly so, for most effect—near your face, but maybe not in your mouth the first time. Crouching over him, I couldn't get a drop out.

Sex is like porn in real life.

After sex in the morning with A. I rush off to work but still arrive late. I tweeted: *If having the best sex of your life is your excuse for anything, don't expect sympathy.* A. was overjoyed when he read that. But it wasn't the best sex of my life; putting it that way made the joke better.

"It doesn't even need a tagline" would be a good tagline for sex.

In Tucson I go home with an old drunk at the bar. He plays several songs on his upright while my head is between his legs. He wants me to spend the night, but I'm feeling regretful about everything and ask for a ride home. When I get back from class the next afternoon, there is a meat thermometer on my doorstep.

My daughter tells me there's no such thing as bad pizza *because bad pizza is even good.*

B. and I are the only couple really getting into it at the open play, rope night. All the other people getting tied up are wearing undergarments; I'm completely nude. No one else is getting whipped and spanked; I'm getting thrashed. None of the other couples are cracking jokes. Spank. Spank. Flog. Wail. Laugh. Spank. Wail. Laugh. Perhaps we are doing it wrong?

I don't give a sex.

M. is embarrassed that I won't take him back after all of his romantic overtures. One night, I wind up at his parent's house in northern Virginia. All I remember about that night is M. made me sleep on the floor because that's where I belonged. We must have been drunk or else I would have left.

Coming down from a low-dose LSD trip in a field outside of Taos, I pee behind B.'s car. While I'm back there, he throws the car into reverse and I jump away, believing I'm about to be backed over. When I finish and climb into the car, he explains to me that he was using the backing cameras to look at my ass. He took a pretty funny picture of it on the rearview camera screen with all the guiding lines; the car thinking B. wanted to parallel park. All I can think is that my ass looks like my mother's.

You know what's sad? When no one releases your sex tape.

L. and I befriend an MFA in fiction at the sex club; the way he fucks we know he's researching a short story.

When I was young and depressed, I just had to ride a motorcycle and have sex with a drummer to get rid of it.

P. was so drunk one night that while eating me out, he stopped to puke over the side of the bed onto the floor. That ruined my self-esteem for a long time while it was also the funniest story about my pussy I told for years.

Twice I had sex and became pregnant.

I watch porn that is a compilation of porn bloopers. In one, a man shoves his cock into a woman's backside. She screams and slaps him away then they both laugh like newscasters as if all he did was read the weather report during the sports highlight reel. So was that not porn? It was a sex mistake? Perhaps following a script is what's pornographic.

While I was pregnant, I practiced safe sex just in case there was the littlest, tiniest, teensiest chance I could get more pregnant.

S. and I live above an Irishman in Richmond whom I had met twice at the mailbox. The third time I meet him, I am wearing stockings and a garter belt under my work skirt. He invites me in to fuck and spank me before my night shift at the diner. I find the setup—that I hardly know him, that our fetishes sync—so interesting that I'm not wet at all. The fucking hurt worse than the spanking.

When we make love, I forget I make 75 cents to your dollar.

R. and I talk about going to a sex club together, but I have never been to one before. It makes me nervous that if we went, I would be inexperienced, I wouldn't understand the protocol, I'd allow things to happen that I may regret later. So, I find one in the city and go alone. I ask the taxi driver to stop at one of those sock stores on St. Marks so I can pick up a pair of thigh-highs and I put them on in the cab. The "club" is really just an apartment party. Everyone congregates in the kitchen. We shake hands with each other and ask, *What do you do?* It was an hour before I started fooling around with a couple. After I go down on the girl while her boyfriend watches, I get the gist and go home.

Sex is never bad until you're not having it.

Your problem is: The choices that you did not make haunt you to the point of anguish.

Zygote

When a woman reads an entire novel in her lap
In one night and the first person she sees
Upon waking is a man.

When a bird shits into a swimming pool
Where a man and woman are swimming.

When a woman breaks three glasses
In three days and on the third day calls her mother

But her mother doesn't answer
Because she was in a car accident.

When a man sends a woman a pen
Through the mail, but the woman

Never opens it because she's out
Purchasing a pregnancy test.

After a woman follows a man to a big city
And lives with him in a small apartment,

The woman
Must eventually get a good job.

When a mommy and daddy love each other
Very much.

When a woman asks a woman
About the kind of yogurt she brought to work last Tuesday

And the second woman begins to cry
Because the first woman is trying so hard to ask something stupid and
normal.

When a woman is very smart.

When a woman is alone.

If you tell me which *Twilight Zone* episode you remember best, I can tell you what your problem is.

"Where is Everybody?"

Your problem is: You cannot reconcile your experiences with what you know of the world, and this causes you to feel powerless.

Substances that Prevent Me From Remembering my Dreams

THC
Alprazolam
Diphenhydramine
MDMA
Diazepam
Alcohol
Psilocybin
Pseudoephedrine
Trazodone
Naltrexone

Nightmare

I dreamed you were dead.
It was v horrible.

They made me give a presentation in your stead
At AWP. And I did, but hyperventilated the whole time

Or I didn't. I can't remember because I was blacked out
With grief. I dreamed you were dead from a Subaru ramming

Itself into the ditch where you had camped.
And when I woke up, sweating, I heard two gunshots

In the alley out back. I dreamed you were dead
And in my dread, I hugged Julia and said, *But he*

Is my oldest friend. I dreamed you were dead
And in the dream, you were my roommate and, while already

Dead, you and I woke up together and I held you
Knowing you were a fantasy, telling you in your ear, *I know you are*

Already dead but this is how I get to hug you one last time.
I hoped you could stick around until Georgia

Moved out. I wondered if I should still mail the package to you
Care of Jen and Jesse in PDX. I texted you, *I hope you are not dead yet*
as of this text.

And you replied, *I am not, as far as I know, though I'd probably be the*
last to know.

Very astute.

To Write

for Camille

To write from the heart or the spine? To write from the heart or the spine. To write words you don't want to read. To read words you don't want to write. To hear words no one wants to hear. To hear anyway and "exquisitely." To write words others may not want to read. To write words others may not want to read and you don't want to hear. To write what others will read and read and read and read and read. To write words you might not want to write. To fuck wanting and write what is needed. To need wanting and write what you don't want. To want nothing and write. To write and want nothing to read. To read inside what others are saying. To read into and underneath what someone is saying to your face. To say to someone's face what is underneath their face. To not do this. To nod. To only nod but never in agreement—

—to nod to get away.

To pray when you don't want to. To put your baby to sleep first though you are exhausted. To always put your baby to sleep first though you are exhausted. To explain when you don't want to teach. To teach when they don't want you to be the one teaching. To teach anyway. To teach by accident. There are no accidents. To listen when you want to read. To listen when you want to talk. To talk when you don't want to. To write when you're not sure if they're listening. Can you ever be sure they aren't listening? To write as you put the baby to bed.

If you tell me which *Twilight Zone* episode you remember best, I can tell you what your problem is.

"A Game of Pool."

Your problem is: You give too much credence to the beliefs others have about your abilities.

Marriage Scene

When I was a new bride,
But not young,

My husband would hide
When I came home.

He didn't work.
He had a profession.

Behind the door first,
The shower curtain soon.

When I began to expect it
Is when it got more scarier.

Beneath the bed next—
How great a place it is from which to slash

An Achilles
Or correct one's grammar,

Much scarier.

Think about nagging
How it turns a woman's pleas

Into vomit,
Something a baby'd do.

How I can't think *wife*
Without all the nagging.

That's...really accurate.

A Funny Thing Happened on the Way to Etel Adnan's Exhibit

My then six-year-old daughter, Georgia, and I arrived in San Francisco for a vacation last Wednesday night. I told her we were going to go to SFMOMA to look at the Etel Adnan paintings the next day and that we should go to City Lights before that, so we could get one of Adnan's books. Maybe we would want to read it while we looked at her paintings.

When we got to the show, Georgia thought the paintings were boring and picked out her favorite one. When we got to the show, I thought the show was small and picked out my favorite one.

I thought, I wonder if I can write about how anything Etel Adnan painted or wrote was funny.

In the Heart of The Heart of Another Country isn't particularly funny and that is the book we bought at City Lights.

But then a funny thing happened on the way to Adnan's exhibit. The show began with a plaque that read:

> Unless otherwise noted, all works:
> Untitled
> 2018
> Oil on canvas

Boring. Small. Very funny.

Is anything possible, I thought.

In her book, *In the Heart of the Heart of Another Country,* Adnan uses the headings and format of William Gass's short story "In the Heart of the Heart of the Country." Adnan wrote, in her book's introduction from Lebanon and to (in her mind) William Gass:

I thought along these lines: So you are in America, and I am here; you may think that you're in trouble, or that there's trouble in your country, but come here and see for yourself the mire into which we're sinking. Just look.[1]

She first picked up his book at City Lights in 1971. There was much unrest and escalating violence in Lebanon in 1971.

Is anything possible, I thought.

In the Heart of the Heart of Another Country begins with a chapter called "In the Heart of the Heart of Another Country." The second chapter is called "Twenty-Five Years Later" and takes the headings and form of the first chapter, recalling it and updating it, in a way.

Adnan's chapter "Twenty-Five Years Later," written twenty-five years after the first, is remarkably funny.

Naming your book *In the Heart of the Heart of Another Country* after a book named *In the Heart of the Heart of the Country* is a lot like having one plaque that says "Untitled, 2018, Oil on canvas" describe twelve to fourteen of your paintings that are hanging in a world-famous museum.

---

[1] Etel Adnan, *In the Heart of The Heart of Another Country* (San Francisco: City Lights Books, 2005), xiii.

58

If you tell me which *Twilight Zone* episode you remember best, I can tell you what your problem is.

The one with the old people who play Kick the Can and become young.

Your problem is: You can remain in the space between action and inaction so long that it causes stasis.

The First Number Will Be a Blues

I like, so much, driving as fast as the car can go.
On a highway in the country. 120 say. It's best if there's a person

With you. Someone you're dating. Maybe you love.
Someone more scared than you are to see you free.

Have you done it in your 40s? You should do it in your 40s.
And if you're too frightened, what you need to do first is go fuck yourself,

Then you'll be able to do it.

In 1955 before his band begins to play *The Blues Walk* the bandleader
Donald Byrd says: "The first number will be a blues."

Don't you love that surety? Will be a blues.
Not: I think we'll play a blues. Not: How about a blues? But: The first number
Will be a blues. And hell if it isn't.

The thing about public land is it's not mine and it's not yours.
It's this third uncomfortable thing, ours.

And things that are ours
Abide rules we learn through others.

Yours and mine rules
Are boring. We're born with them.

The first number is one.
And it will be a blues.

You don't have to tell me twice.
The pain I see in my child
Is my mother's and I am the bridge.

Another poet might tell you about all the research she's done
On Donald Byrd. She'd wedge Byrd's

Life in here
As allegory or, something worse,

Metaphor.

Before we're born, my mother tells us,
We watch movies of every life we could be born into. Then we choose.

The little baby points from her astral cradle. That one.
I choose that mama.
I choose that daddy.

I choose that irrevocably broken marriage,
That accident that wires my jaw shut,
That burned popcorn, that daughter late in life named Georgia,
That root canal, that unending night on mushrooms,
That dog bite, that last beer with Oren,
That A+, that DUI, that refrigerator stinking of rotten eggs
Because I don't have enough for the electric bill.

It's like you're inside my head!!!!

People I've Gone to the Movies With

Alison	Andrew
Nikki	Khadijah
Casey	Tariq
Georgia	Andre
Toni	Ron
Greg	Debbie
Nina	Nicholas
Gwen	Jaime
Matt	Andy
Oren	Greg
Brian	Sarah B.
Elisa	Phil
Eric	Abby
Andrea	Mathias
Poppy	Noah
Paul	Jon
Sam	Sarah M.
Amy	Brenna
Martin	Kelly
Arianne	Kristina
Karl	Alex
David	Stephanie
Julie	Adrienne
Amy	Robert
Julia	Josh
Sophia	Jamal
Tony	Shannon
Serena	Kasey

If you tell me which *Twilight Zone* episode you remember best, I can tell you what your problem is.

The one where the kids play hide and seek with their 'special' baby-sitter guy, and one kid gets bit by a dog, and when it's the babysitter's turn to hide, he hides inside a scarecrow, and the vigilantes find him after they erroneously think he hurt the kids. Yuck.

I don't know this one.

The American Night is Young

It has been 45 years
Since I've come home
From the hospital.

I left to pick up milk
And never came back.

I think about getting killed
By a dune buggy.

I care little
For shame.

You were happy until
You weren't.

You are
Until you aren't.

A lover's mouth in your ear
Isn't a wet willy,

It's communication.

A little like love.
A little like buying a lover a plane ticket.

If you tell me which *Twilight Zone* episode you remember best, I can tell you what your problem is.

The one where Charles Bronson eats fried chicken out of a can in a post-apocalyptic world.

Your problem is: You believe that you can never fully know another, and this prevents you from offering unconditional love.

Life: A Draft

Fuck traffic.

Fuck cars.

Fuck steak.

Fuck Wendy's.

Fuck a foam soap.

Fuck media.

Have you seen the moon tonight? It fucking sucks.

Fuck texting.

Fuck us.

Fuck *No worries.*

Fuck waiting in line.

How hard is it to fucking reply all?

Fuck diets.

Fuck electricity.

Fuck sex.

Fuck higher education.

Fuck air travel.

Often I am permitted to return to a meadow and I don't know what the fuck to do when I get there.

Fuck cinema.

Fuck bottled water.

Fuck this.

Fuck that.

Time's all like, *Fuck you.*

Why did the porn star get fired? She didn't give a fuck.

Fuck jokes.

Fuck television.

What a [fucking] piece of work is a man.

Sigh.

Single Mom

I want to make the mistakes
Famous people make:

    · Divorcing in underpants
    · Lighting a crack cigarette
    · Getting fat

I want to make these mistakes so well
That I am offered a part
In the movie
Of the story
Of *My Life*
By Lyn Hejinian.

Into-an-Empty-Swimming-Pool-Diving in Love

I think *Grey Gardens* (1975) is a perfect movie. It also happens to be good. *Grey Gardens* is a documentary about a mother and a daughter, both defunct relatives of Jacqueline Kennedy Onassis, and their poverty-stricken lives in a run-down mansion called Grey Gardens. They are both named Edith, but the mother is called Big Edie and the daughter, Little Edie. There is no movie more about women than this movie. This movie is about what happens when women are permitted to become feral. What happens when women are permitted to revel in their own psychology and plumb it (plummet), free from some parts of the panopticon. I see in these women my entire life, not the details of course, but a thick layer of it: the worries and obsessions and deep connections and fluctuating esteem.

When Little Edie talks about feeling trapped at Grey Gardens, Big Edie says to her, *You can't get any freedom when you're being supported.*

Little Edie says, *I think you're not free when you're not being supported.*

Then a bit later Little Edie adds: *It's awful both ways.*

I write in a poem about an old friend named Melissa naming her daughter Melissa. *How patriarchal,* I say in the poem, acknowledging that because Melissa and Melissa are women, this act is, in reality, radically anti-patriarchal.

Friday night, Sara and Mary Jane talked with me about the names in their families. Sara is named after her grandmother. Sara says her aunts would call each other Mary or Mare, though none of them were named Mary. Mary stood for girl. Hey Mare. Hey girlfriend. Hey girl.

My mother called my sister and me, her little girlfriends. *Mama's little girlfriend,* she would singsong when we were feverish while she traced her fingers on our foreheads.

I call my daughter, friend. *Friend, can you help me in the kitchen? Did you have any dreams last night, friend?*

Roy told us by the fire, Friday night, that his mother's name was Leelah and that his middle name is Lee. He said he hates that middle name but not because of his mother. Because of a man named Lee. When he told us his parents were slaves everyone went quiet.

I wish I could have told Roy that Lee was Jackie Kennedy's middle name, too. But I learned that today. And today is a few days after Friday.

Little Edie says, *It's very difficult to keep the line between the past and the present.*

Sometimes I cannot point out one boundary between Big Edie and her daughter, Little Edie.

That night by the fire with Roy I remarked that Leelah is such a lovely and rare name. But there are other Leelahs. Leelah Alcorn is a young woman who walked into traffic because she was alone and alienated and condemned for being transgender. She had no support. She had no freedom.

I think you're not free when you're not being supported, Little Edie said. And that, that is the boundary between Big Edie and Little Edie, between mother and daughter, between past and present.

You're free when you're supported.

You're free when you're supported.

We measure love until everyone has it.

Sommer, what's your favorite episode, & what's your problem?

Dramatis Personae

mother	Toni Browning
sister	Casey Browning
daughter	Georgia Browning
father	Martin Browning

The one where the kids swim to the bottom of their pool and come up at a lake with a warm and loving grandma type, but then they have to swim back to their shit lives.

Where Anthony turns the guy into the jack in the box, and Anthony wishes him into the cornfield.

"Black leather jackets."

The one where the mannequins in the department store come to life.

"The Good Life." The young child who has mental powers over everyone and terrorizes them.

The one where the test pilot/astronauts slowly become erased from existence, one by one, after flying an experimental space-plane, "And When the Sky Was Opened."

The one with the disfigured patient who turns out to be perfectly attractive as compared to the pig-faced medical team treating them.

Guy tosses coin in change bucket, and it lands on its edge, then he can read people's minds. He later goes back and knocks it over. "Penny For Your Thoughts."

The one with Shatner, obviously.

The one where two guys are going through a desert with gold and trying to survive, and the end shows that gold isn't worth anything anymore because they can manufacture it.

"The Midnight Sun," 1961.

The one where everyone is afraid of the little boy/son because he can make anything happen with his mind. They cater to him, and he just threatens to turn them into weird things.

"Jess-Belle."

The one with the evil ventriloquist's dummy!

The one where people go back in time and take your things but put them back before you notice but somewhere else.

I can't remember any of them bc I have neurological problems.

The one where Dennis Hopper is a neo-Nazi & begins getting advice from Hitler.

The one with the man on trial who is innocent and relives every day and then screams "look in the oven!" at the prosecutor who finds out too late the man was right after he sees there's a turkey in there like he promised.

Your problem is: You hold yourself to an ideal that is impossible to attain, and this causes suffering.

Your problem is: You compare your successes to those of others rather than examining them in your own life's context, and this causes suffering.

Your problem is: Intellectually, you know you determine your own course, but you do not feel that is the case, and this causes pain.

Your problem is: You give too much credence to how others view you, and this causes ambivalence.

Your problem is: You distrust your perception of the world and rightly believe that it is a veil, but this causes indecision to the point of anxiety.

Your problem is: The fact that intuition and logic can be in conflict makes you doubt the value of both, and this torments you.

Your problem is: When destructive patterns of thinking you have left behind prove useful, you doubt yourself, and this causes misery.

Your problem is: You're hesitant to express your desires and fears in the moment and often believe you have missed your chance, and this causes you sorrow.

Your problem is: You fear both risk-taking and planning, because you erroneously believe they are oppositional.

Your problem is: You suffer when you reject the idea that reality is a many-layered construction, much of it out of your control.

Your problem is: Your perception of the world and your experiences do not align, and this causes you to distrust your desires.

Your problem is: You believe truth is subjective, and this causes you to doubt your desires which makes you rigid.

Your problem is: You use one standard to evaluate the behavior of others and another to evaluate your own, and this causes you difficulty in relationships.

Your problem is: You see your successes on a spectrum but your failures as immutable, when neither is true.

Your problem is: Your received values conflict with your knowledge. You know this yet align your goals with them, making them impossible to achieve.

Your problem is: You hold back from intimacy, because you believe there is an unbridgeable abyss between people.

Your problem is: You believe in the truth of action over the truth of feeling, when neither is accurate, and this causes you great pain.

Your problem is: You despair when you believe there is a difference between your voice and truth.

Wow! I think that's true. Not sure how you got that from this, though.

I Miss

Your black air.
Your okes.
How you'd ext me
Thoughts, to do ists.
I miss
Calling you riend.
Your ongue.
My hands flat
Against your ack.
Your ands against
ine.

If you tell me which *Twilight Zone* episode you remember best, I can tell you what your problem is.

I think the only episode I've seen is "Midnight Sun," where the earth spun out of its orbit and is moving closer to the sun. It is very vivid in my memory.

Your problem is: The contradiction between how you feel and what you know can immobilize you to the point of suffering.

The Briefest Interview in the World

If you could ask 30 people to answer one question, what would it be?

What were your first formative political experiences from childhood?

Wendy C. Ortiz

What's an object from your childhood that you wish you still had?

Elisa Gabbert

I'd want to know the most embarrassing thing they ever did!!

Sueyeun Juliette Lee

How do you live through and with pain?

Khadijah Queen

Seattle?

Graham Foust, in a dream

How are we going to help the kids rebuild after this is over?

Camille Dungy

What is your favorite color to wear?

Kazim Ali

Why do you think mating for life with one person is a good idea?

The Cyborg Jillian Weise

What do ghosts know that we don't?

Selah Saterstrom

Can you name one or two times that someone has been radically kind to you, like really gone out of their way to do some super kind shit for you?

Steven Dunn

Have you got any good dirt on the other 29 people on this list?

Larry Hama

What's the last thing you photographed?

Eduardo C. Corral

What was the happiest day of your life?

Thor Harris

If you could ask 30 people to answer one question, what would it be?

Georgia Browning

What do you know about indigenous sovereignty?

Erika T. Wurth

What is your confession to the maple tree?

Cynthia Arrieu-King

What was the absolute happiest moment of your life?

David Heska Wanbli Weiden

If you could only pick one of the following, which do you think would
most ably guide you to a better life? Good politics, good ethics, or good
aesthetics?

Tony Tost

Do you love me, and why?

Ana Božičević

What do you wish you had known when you were 15?

Stephanie Burt

What is the first sound you remember falling in love with?

Hanif Abdurraqib

If you think about something that you love to do, like when you do it,
you're fully engaged in it, can you remember the first time you felt that,
the first time you knew it would be something you love to do?

Mary-Kim Arnold

How old were you the first time you fell in love?

Nikki Wallschlaeger

What is one lesson you've learned in life that you wished you'd learned earlier?

Ani Cordero

If you had to make up one word for your favorite thought, what would that word be and how would you describe that thought?

Serena Chopra

What do you think your reason is for existing?

Tommy Guerrero

What was the first text you read that made you aware that there was a self in you that you had yet to realize?

Sina Queyras

I find it important, utterly critical, to ask myself, at least every day: Am I wrong?

Chase Berggrun

What does utopia—based purely on a positive vision, on what you DO want, not based on or responding to what you don't want—look like to you?

Conner Habib

What would be better.

Joyelle McSweeney

If you tell me which *Twilight Zone* episode you remember best, I can tell you what your problem is.

What if I can't tell if what I'm remembering is a Twilight Zone *or* Fantasy Island *episode?*

Oral History

I can't even tell you what happened today.

I put on a Yes record. In fact, I think it was
The Yes Album.
(It's still playing.)

Of course,
There was a lot of suffering today:

Whitney's, Philip's, K's.
I sat on the porch and remembered

Being 41
Sneaking out of the house

Into an amateur porn actor's van
(You know those vans?)

And giving him the longest handjob in the world.

He looked at me like I was his mother—
I insisted he call me

Professor.
I'm proud of it really

Because I make a lot of friends
Laugh when I recount the story.

My arm ached for days, I say.
Boy, Sommer, that's—

Funny. Sure,
Some of them feel weird listening to it,

But that's because

They secretly
Dropped out of poetry school.

Turns out it was Fantasy Island.

Thank You For Playing[1]

Darryl Lorenzo Wellington, Maggie Golston, Lisa Biever, Nathan Lipke, Lauren Crain Bender, Gary Remer, William Leonard Valdez, Lisa Howe, Nate Maxson, Mike Huff, Karl Chwe, T Edward Bak, Sherine Gilmour, Sydney Justine Simpson, Ron Miller, Nik De Dominic, Elder Zamora, Cynthia Gallaher, Paula Cisewksi, Kathleen Rooney, Robin Thompson, David S. Atkinson, Reuben Jackson, Carol Elaine, Jaimie Rudy, Kristin Bock, Katie Jean Shinkle, Susan Rowland, Tim Earley, Camille Dungy, Carter Monroe, Paul Bilger, Katrina Helene, Glenn A. Bruce, Daniel Tiffany, Donna Robertson Swanson, Curtis Romero, Gillian Devereux, Alyse Knorr, Kevin O'Connell, Nate Logan, Judith Miller, Larry Hama, Aubrey Lenahan, Randall Meehl, Caitie Drost, Sue Spengler, Christina Homer, David Eingorn, A. O. Dugas, Harry Kollatz Jr., Robin Lindley, Quintan Ana Wikswo, Stephen Masters, Deborah Phelps, Moisés B Rodriguez, Erik Mortenson, Matthew Rudnicki, Jacob S. Knabb, Andrew Topel, Daisy McGowan, Jason Guard, Shawn Angel, Krystal Languell, Ana Božičević, Wendy C. Ortiz, @acoppa, @matagott, Lauren Gifford, Jennifer Martelli, Julianna Walsh, @New_Dork, Cary Barbor, Leo Levinsky, Rebecca Loudon, @StormLegacyTeam, Joanna Penn Cooper, Alex Everette, @RWWrites, Chris Wells, Cara Benson, Fred Schmalz, @DrThomasMorrow, J. Mae Barizo, Manuel Aragon, @probablyalissa, Dillon Hawkins, Mary McHugh, @smwenk, Magdalena Zurawski, Joseph Mosconi, Anna Vangala Jones, Annabelle Bronstein, Laurie Hertzler, @MoyruhJo, Collin Treviño Bost, @jrkjrkjrkjrk, Clay Landon, @EPapp2000, Andra Moldav, @JunkyardAttic, Alex LaGrand, Will Walawender, Amy Lawless, Kristen Arnett, Nathan Pensky, Rachel Springer, Jess Saiyan, Joe Nanni, @CooperWilhelm, @IAmGoldenHolden, Bryan J. Pitchford, @ScriberEstAgere, Courtney Clute, Maureen O'Connor Saringer, Casey Rocheteau, @dragphotog, Renée Branum, Mark Reels, @TLBREIT, @monapily, Toni Judnitch, @megandalland, @suezette, @chadbtp, Cheshire Adams, Kathryn Tuggle, @RacheyForReals, @DaGirv, John Rice, Cody DeMatteis, @goatfalcon, @tomato_square, @wealthy_person, Cheryl Pappas, Ben Tanzer, @itsAnnXiety, Anthony Michael Morena, Sequoia Nagamatsu, @backpackbunny, Melissa Pena, Keisha-Gaye Anderson, @PinkHerring, @kaaaylaaag, Heather Green, Lina Skandalakis, @smolgayslam, Summer Block, Laura Scalzo, Kate Abbott, Dave Harrison, Peter Stuart Lakanen, @TCBGP, J.A. Tyler, Jason Powell, Mark Leidner, @noahfs50540, Safia James, Cameron Finch, @npiombino, @etwurth, @rlkokay, @brendanistan, @Diurnalprimate, @matthewzapruder,

---

[1] *Part of this book is a textual Rorschach test I conducted over several days on Twitter and Facebook. I asked, If you tell me which Twilight Zone episode you remember best, I can tell you what your problem is. I engaged with hundreds of people, writing each one of them a therapy-fueled aphorism that "diagnosed" their "problem" inspired by their remembered episode.*

@SirHardHarry, @WriteLauraBond, @mt_pages, @tunnelscreech, @nikkiwpowell, @dedreytnien, @Spencer_Short, @LinesOfForce, @MattSeccombe1, @ambernoelle, @alexisnomi, @joshuabohnsack, @JoymoorMoor, @JoanSGarofalo, @_ashtart_, @blaiseallysen, @ClaireKirchMN, @blondebudda, @bjnovak, @jen_sparkles, @bbcinani, @ButtersV2, @usefuljack, @RhiBWay, @leighannzig, @planningforever, @WGladstone, @BolognaE, @IAmKatyLees, @KolleenCarney, @guyincognito, @kfan, @donnahoke, @kimkimanton, @wendyar, @bloodyserb, @ReginaKrystyn, @slipperyredhead, @LizLabunski, @sorenrhett, @LGatesMarkel, @karltaro, @ZaraLisbon, @justin_karcher, Adjua Gargi Nzinga Greaves, Terrence Folz, Donatello Fodness, Matt Jasper, Timothy Donnelly, Mary-Henry Marcus, Kasey Mohammad, Hannah Rebecca Gamble, Stephanie Michelle Cleveland, Renee Catkin, Christopher Michael, Ed Scott, Lisa Marie Basile, Christopher Verdak, Chavisa Woods, Alicia E Vasquez, Lisa O'Neill, Harmoni Mcglothlin, and Erik Grotz.

Acknowledgements

I would like to thank Patrick Pethybridge, Anselm Berrigan, Rachel Franklin Wood, Evelyn Hampton, Bailey Pittenger, ari k. castañeda, Karen An-hwei Lee, Elle Nash, rob mclennan, Elizabeth Scanlon, Jessica Lowenthal, Christopher Dyer, Emily Pettit, Lindsay Turner, Walt Hunter, Joseph Young, and Adam Robinson for including some of the work in this book in the following: *pulpmouth, The Brooklyn Rail, Visible Binary, Witch Craft Magazine, periodicities, American Poetry Review, Jacket2, Mother Damnable, jubilat, Small House Pamphlet Series, Everyone Quarterly.*

People are the best thing in my life. I am deeply grateful for the love, support, vital encouragement, and incredible brains of Mathias Svalina, Julia Cohen, Joshua Ware, Noel Black, The Cyborg Jillian Weise, Miriam Benatti, Alison Walsh, Nikki McKnight, Sueyeun Juliette Lee, Amy Vidali, Elisa Gabbert, Erin Costello, Jeanne Liotta, David Shields, Chris Tonelli, Justin Marks, Toni Browning, Casey Browning, Georgia Eli Browning, and Martin Browning.

Photo and DETH LIGHGHT t-shirt by Joshua Ware taken at GEORGIA, Denver in front of Sol LeWitt's *Wall Drawing #797*.

Sommer Browning is a poet and writer living in Denver. This is her third collection of poetry.